MAZE

Vol 6

Ages 4-6

FOR KIDS

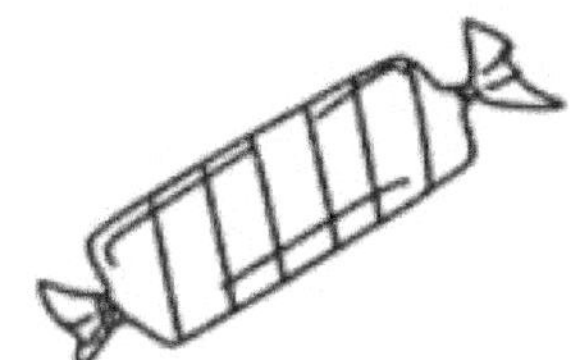

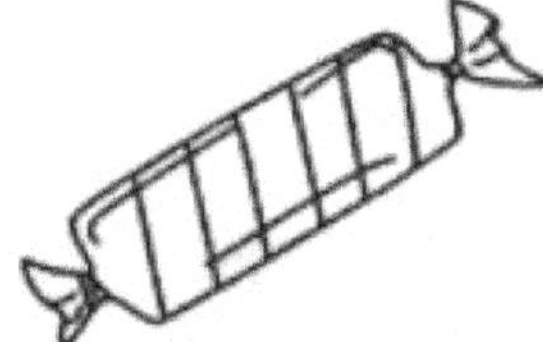

MAZE BOOK

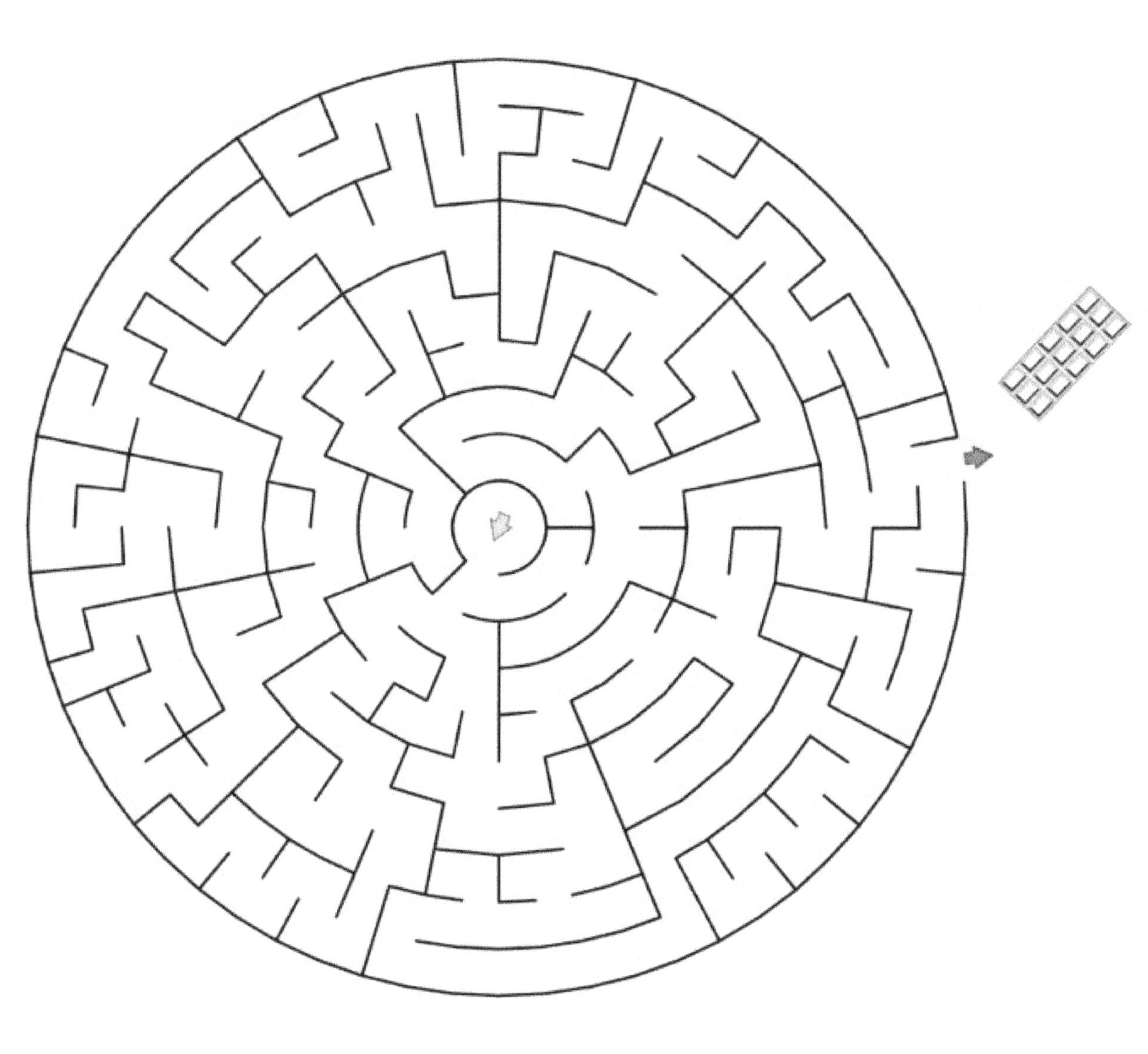

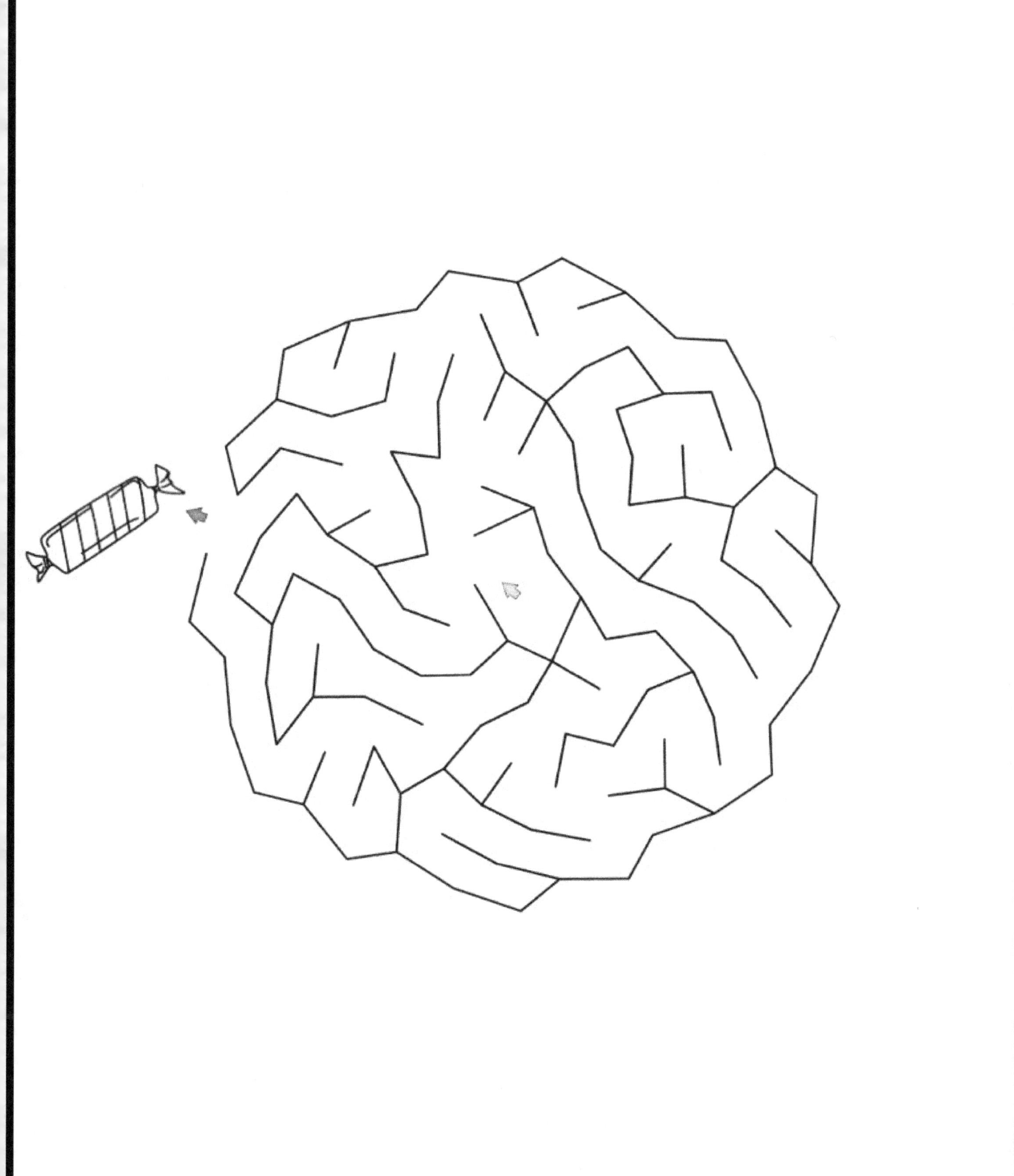

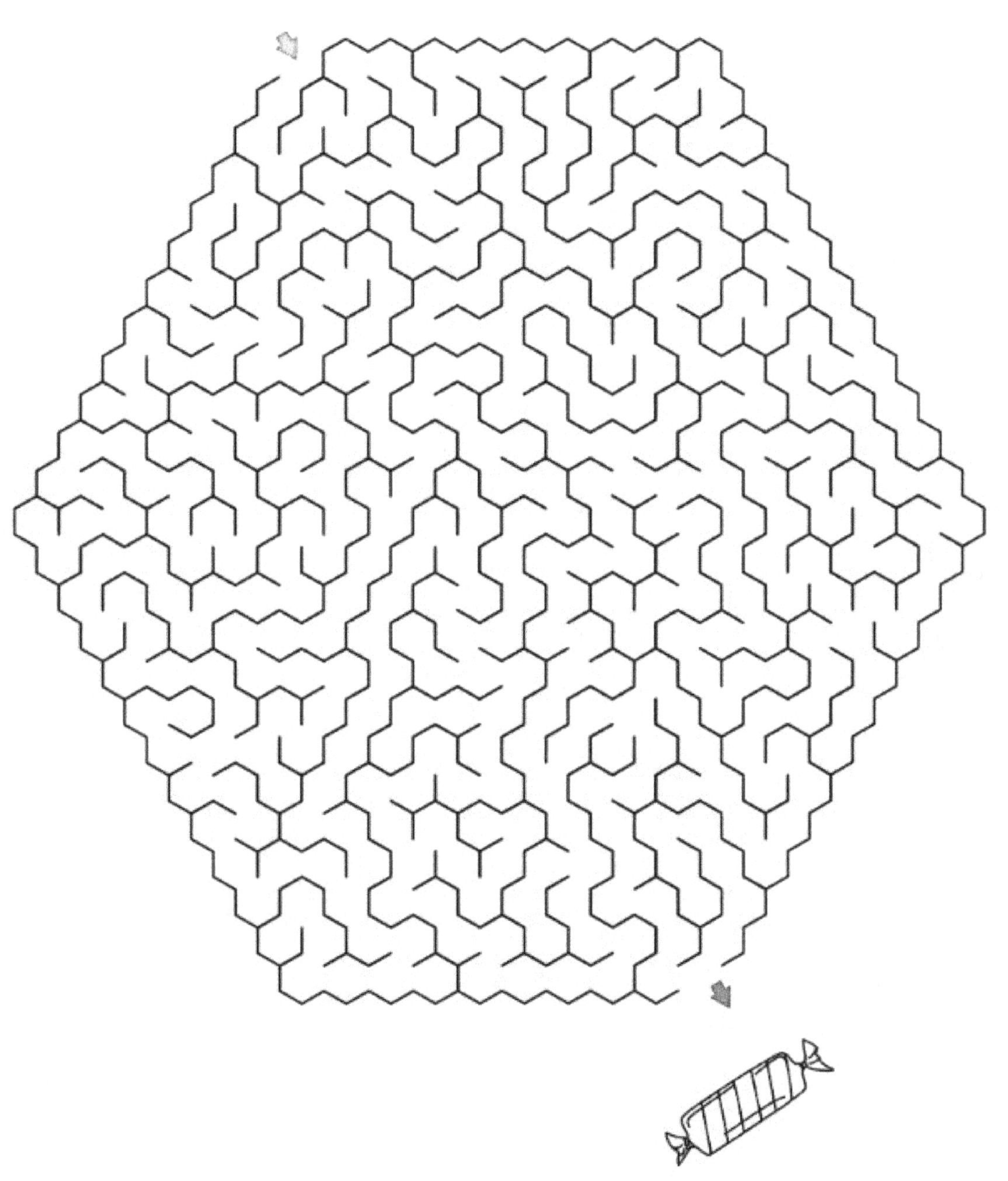

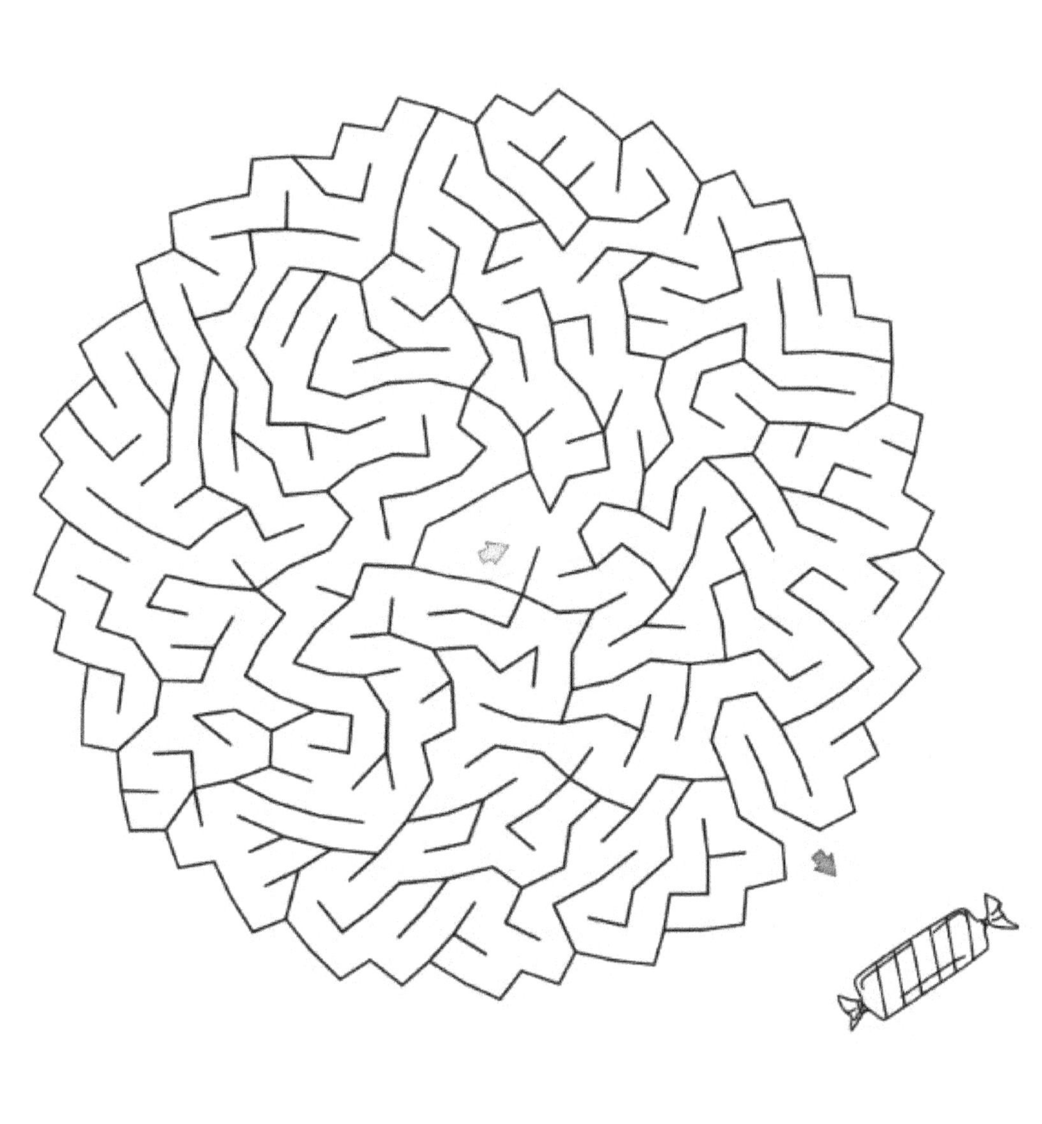

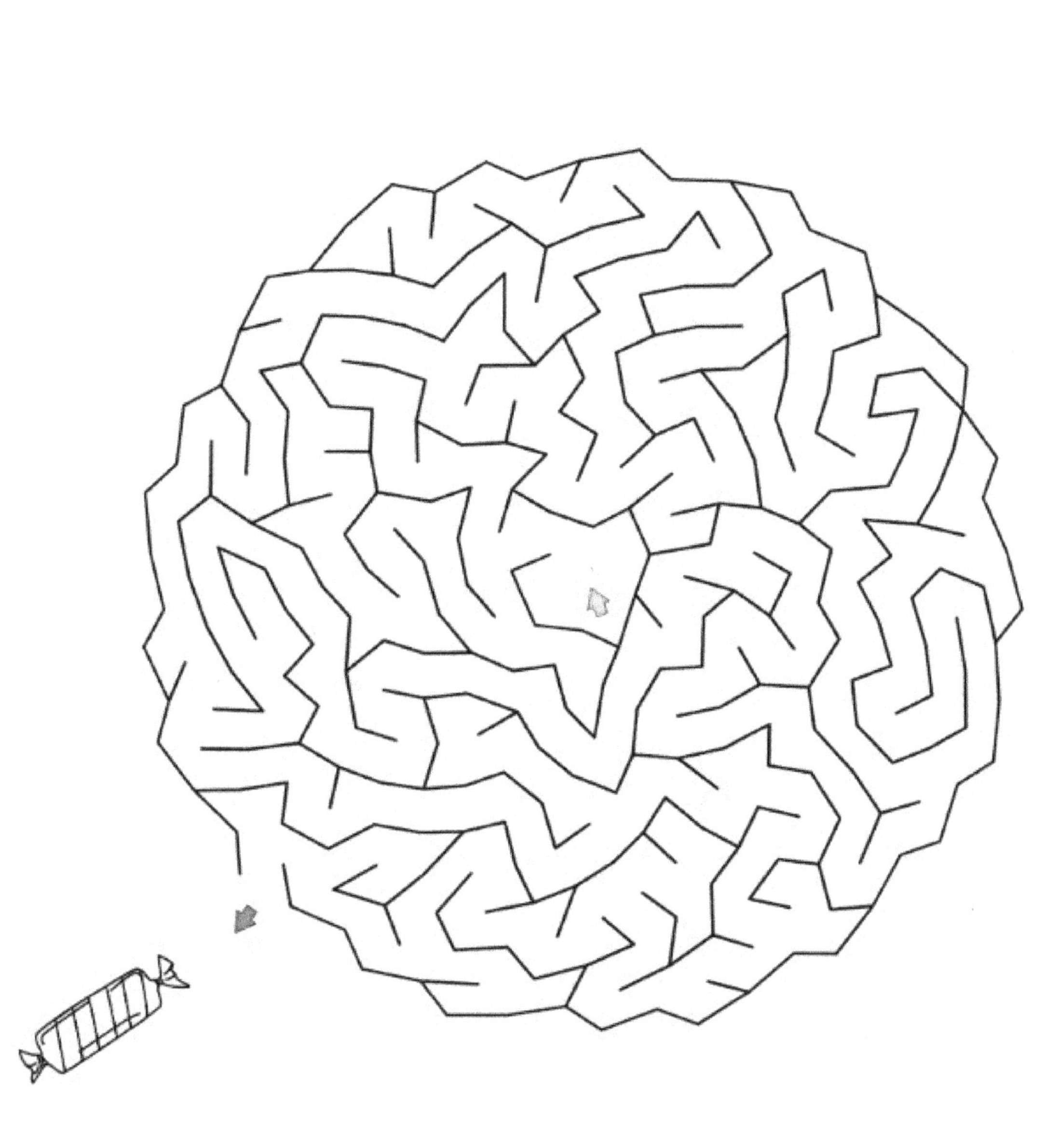

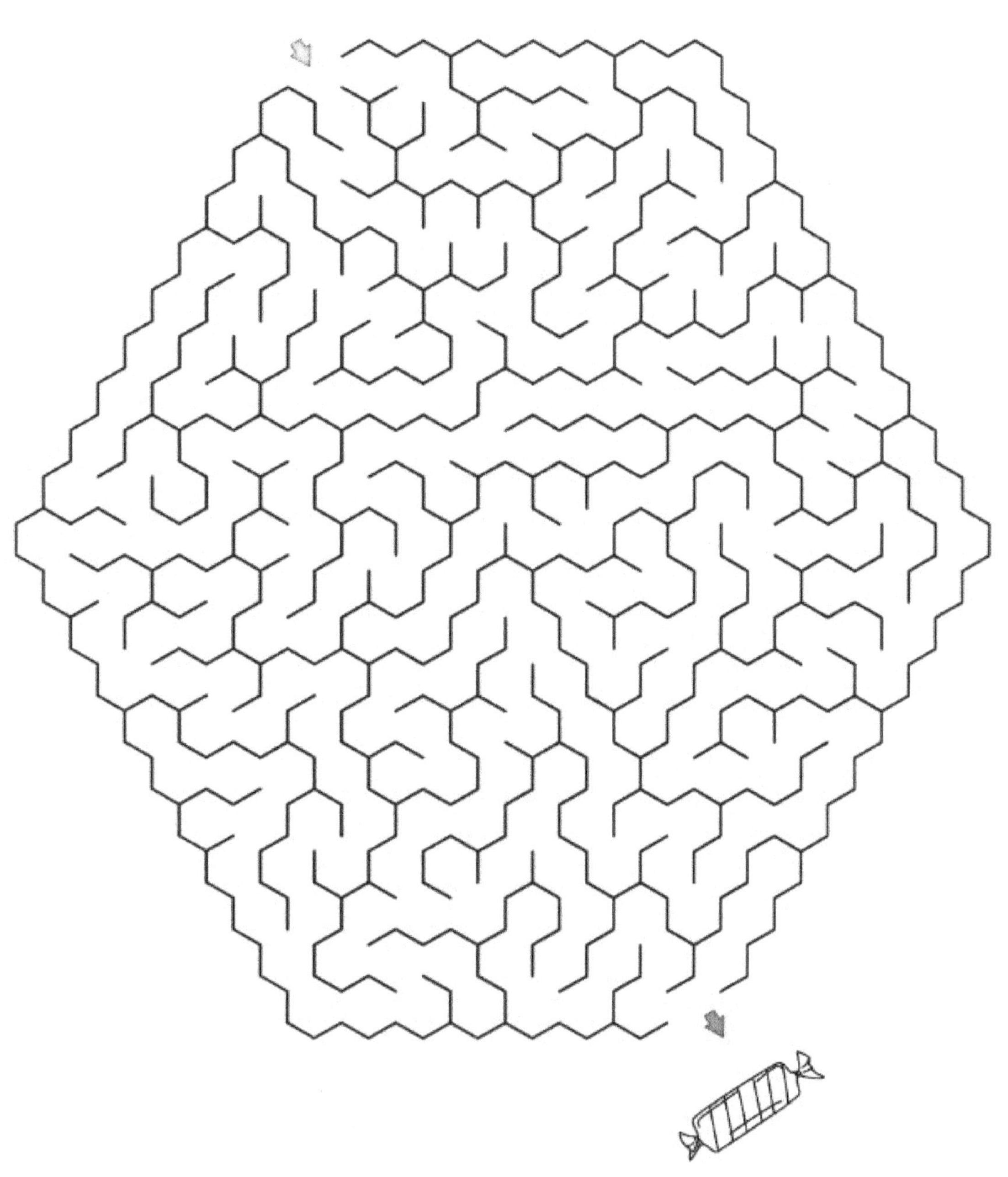

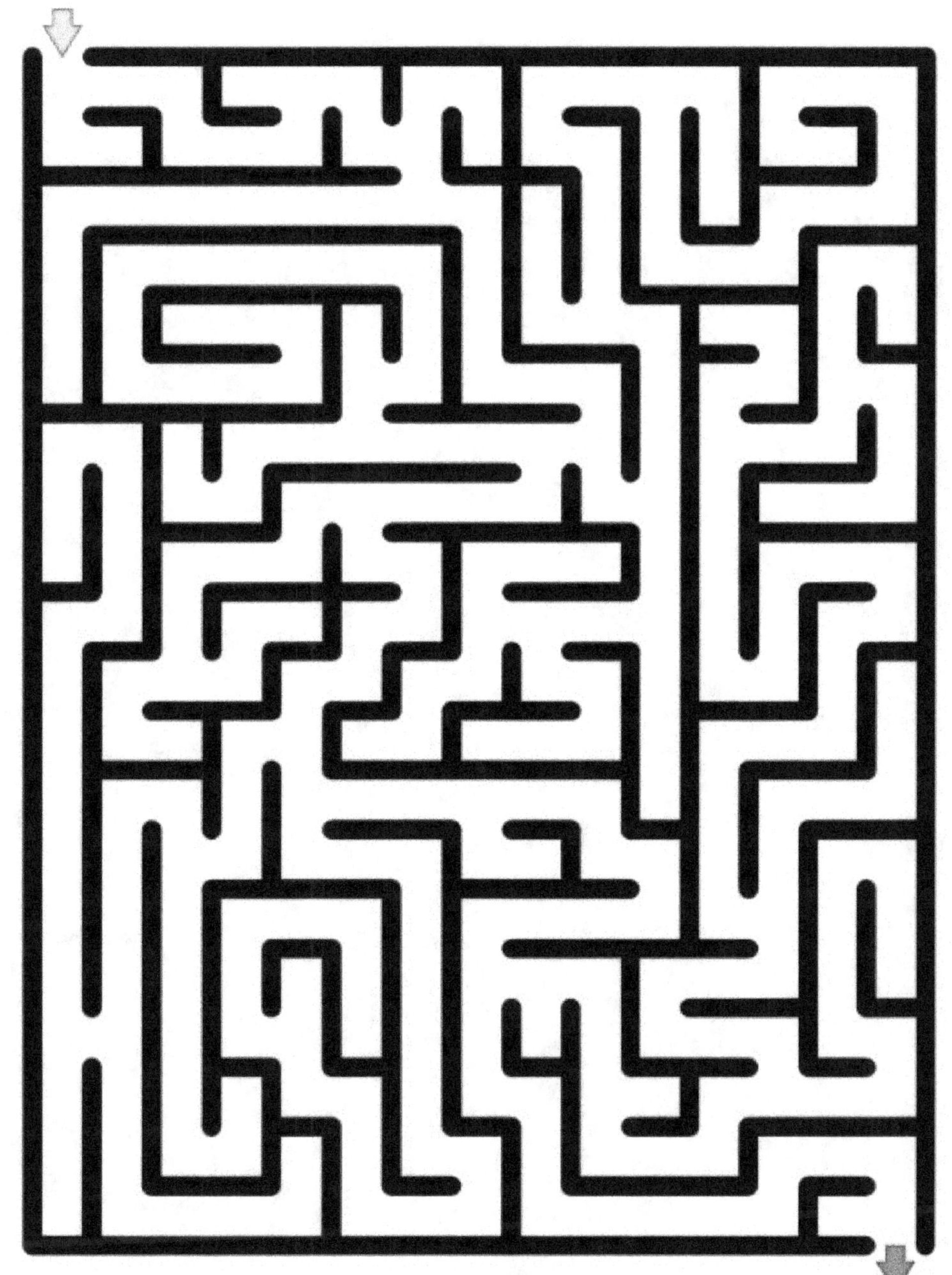

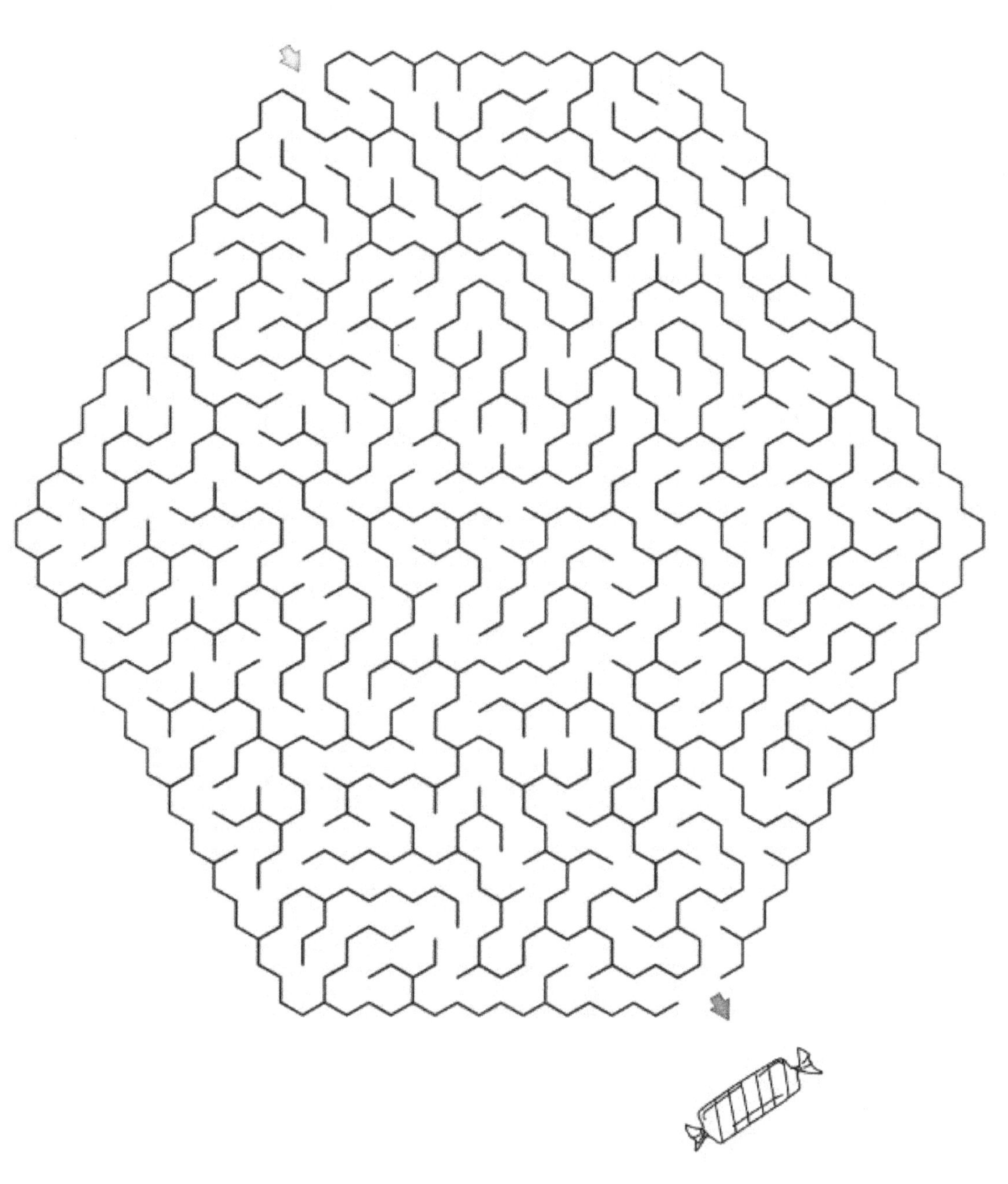

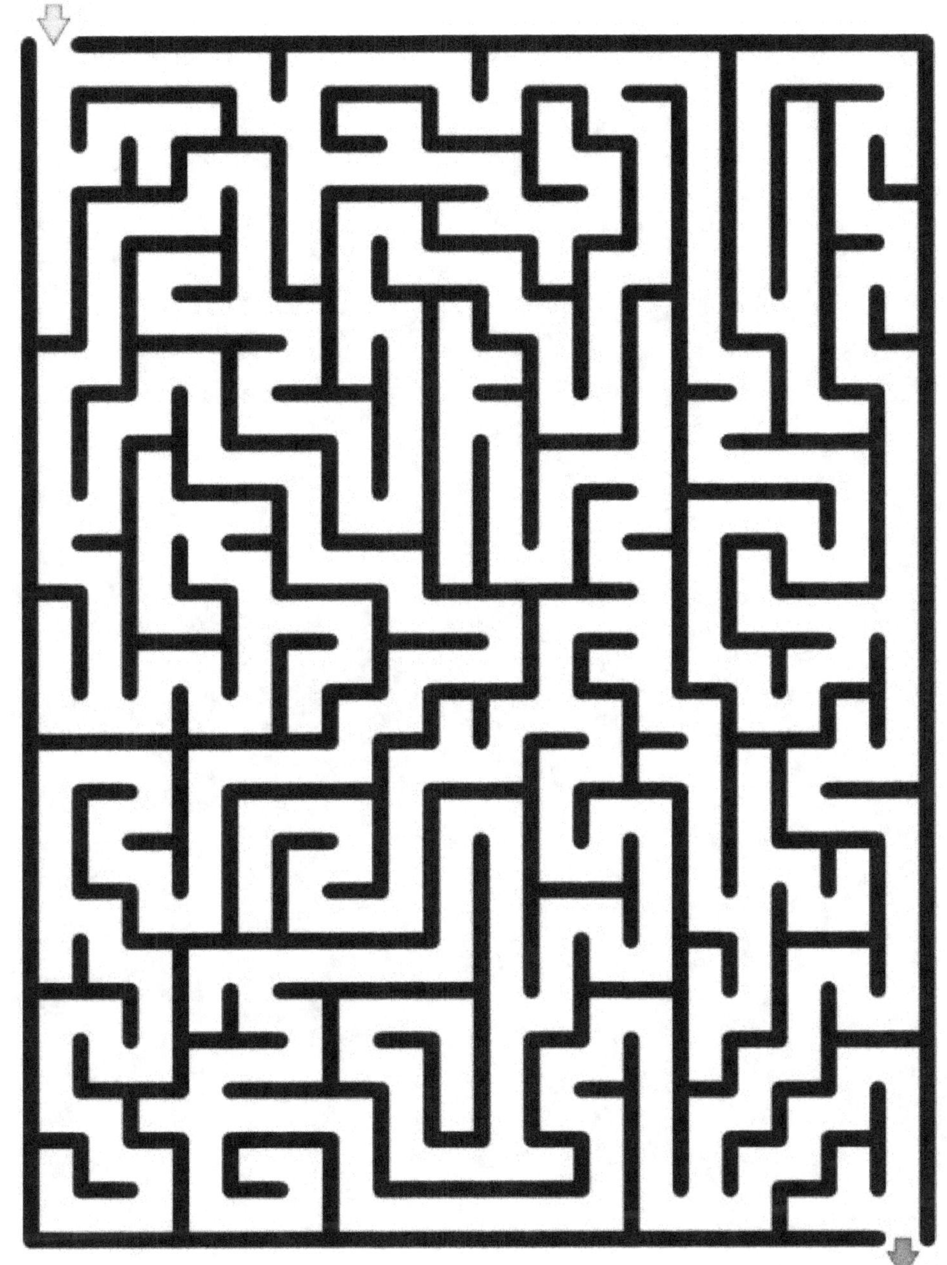

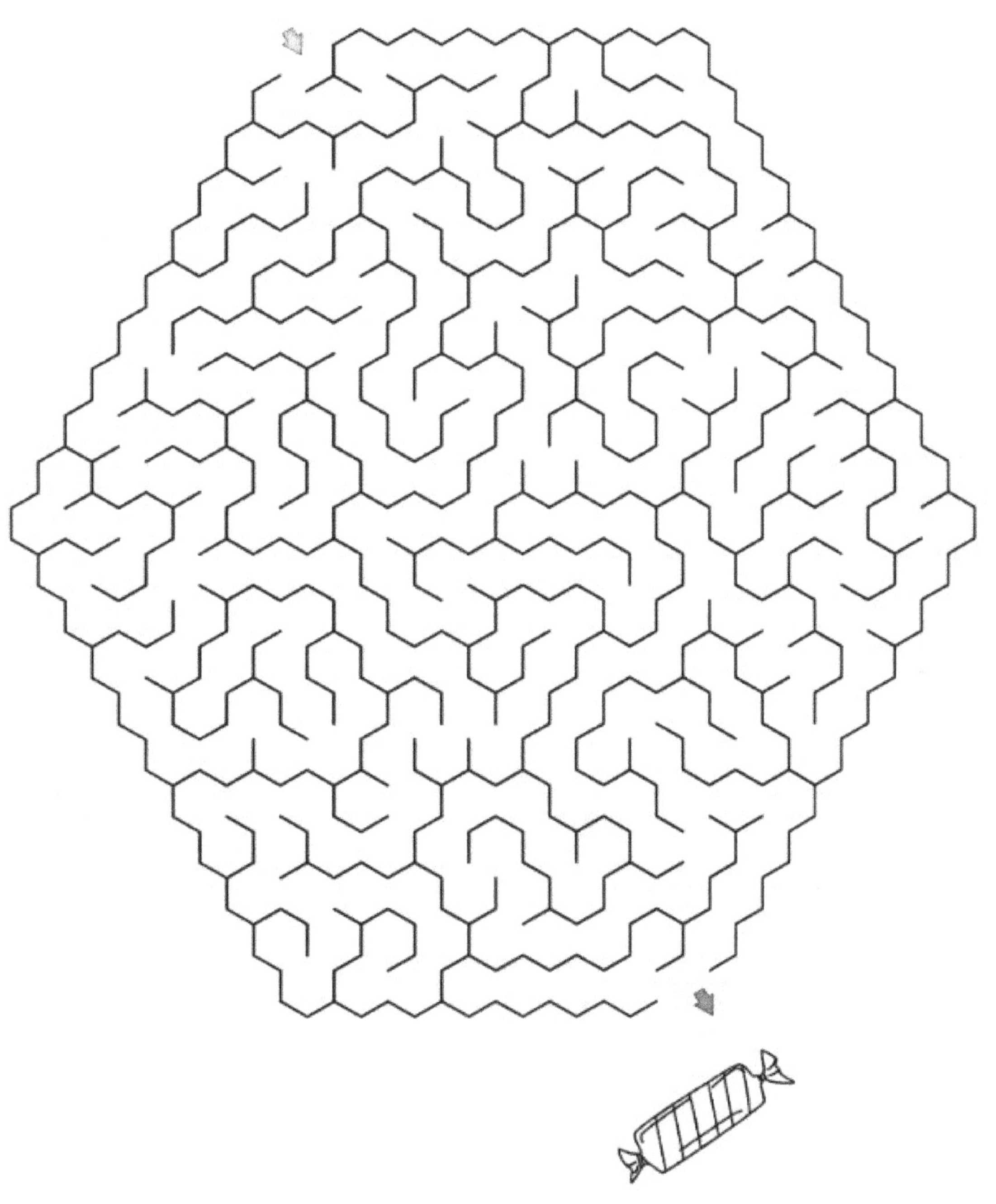

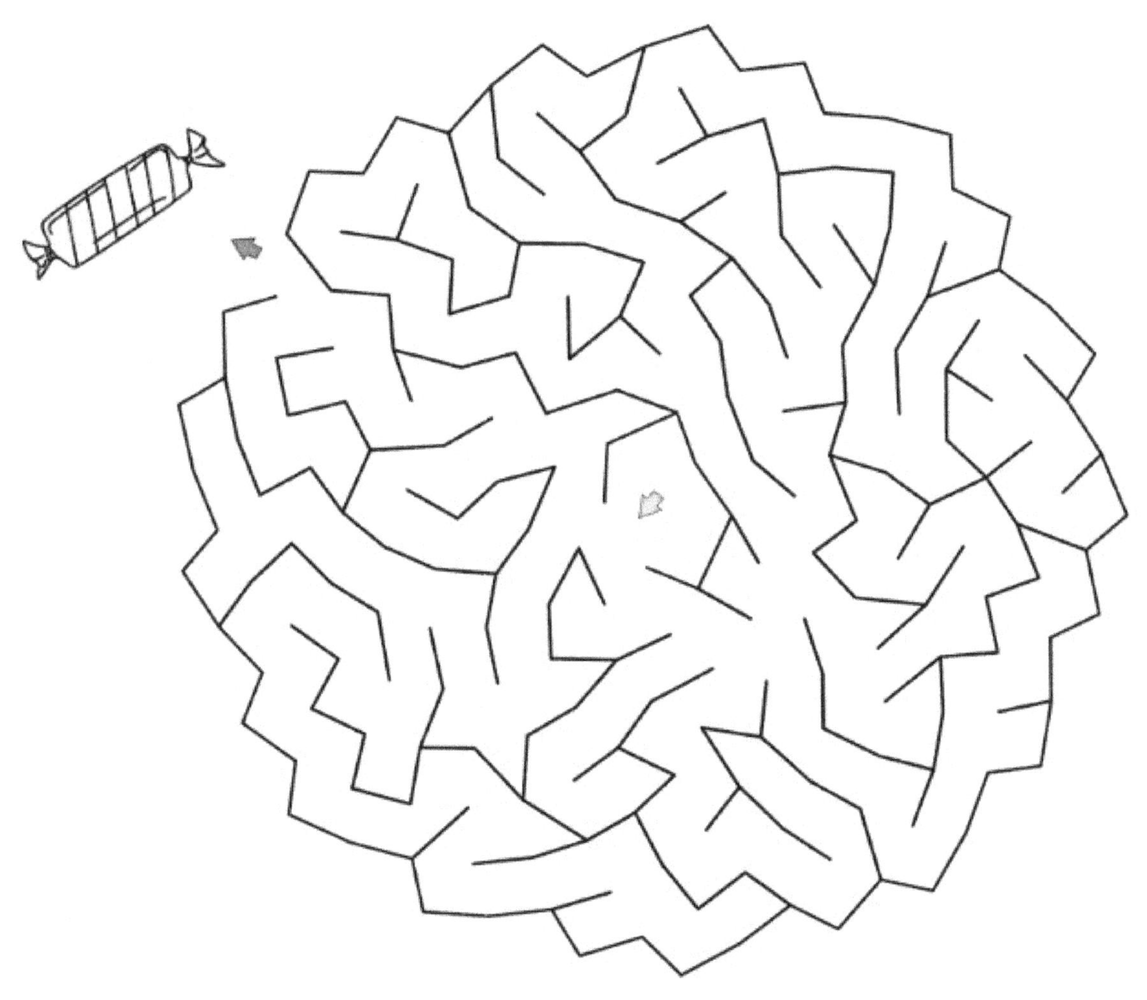

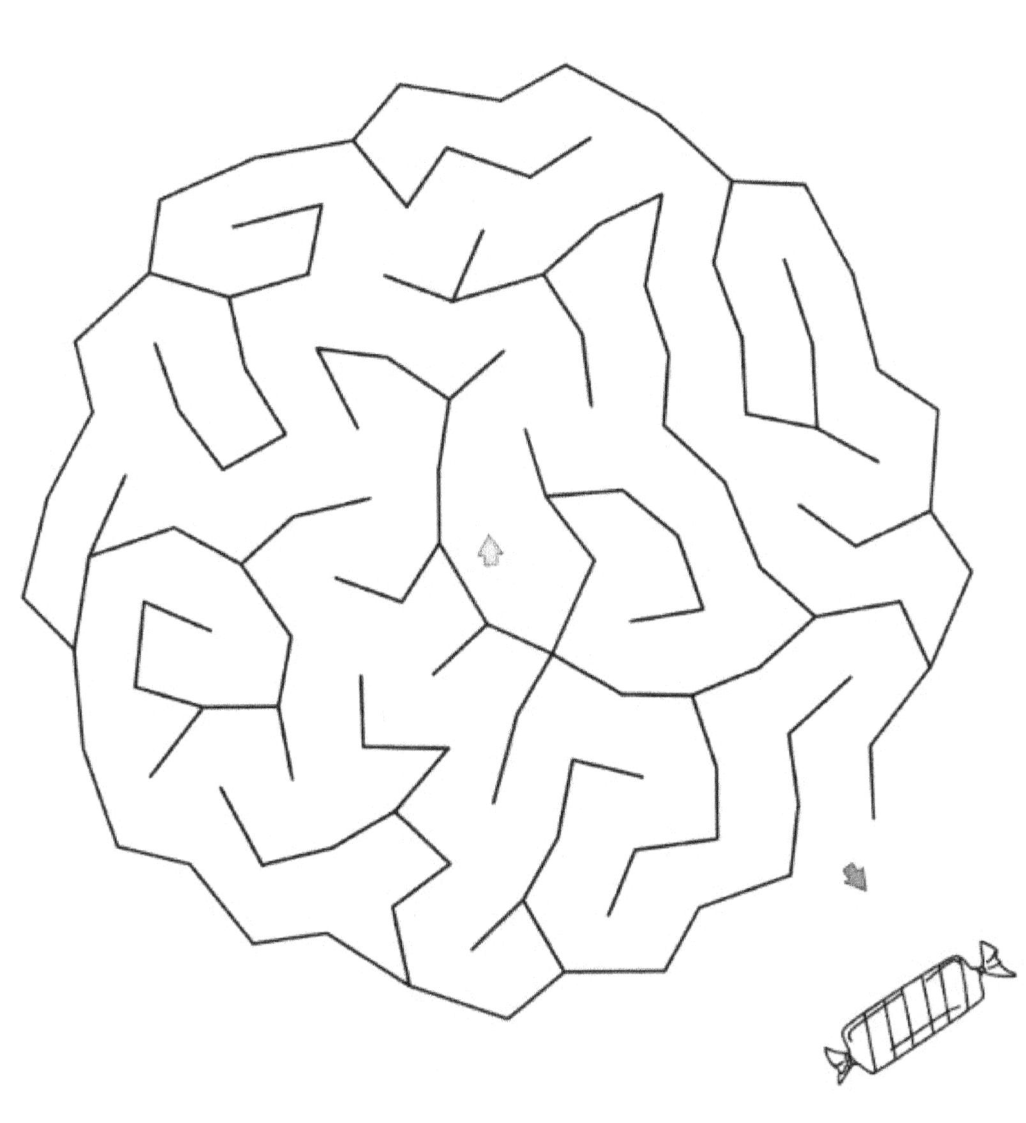